# WAKE

**Gillian Allnutt** was born in 1949 in London but spent half of her childhood in Newcastle upon Tyne. In 1988 she returned to live in the North East. Before that, she read Philosophy and English at Cambridge and then spent the next 17 years living mostly in London, working mostly as a part-time teacher in further and adult education but also as a performer, publisher, journalist and freelance editor. From 1983 to 1988 she was Poetry Editor at *City Limits* magazine.

Her collections *Nantucket and the Angel* and *Lintel* were both shortlisted for the T.S. Eliot Prize. Poems from these collections are included in her Bloodaxe retrospective *How the Bicycle Shone: New & Selected Poems* (2007), which draws on six published books plus a new collection, *Wolf Light*, and was a Poetry Book Society Special Commendation. Her most recent collections, both from Bloodaxe, are *indwelling* (2013) and *wake* (2018). She has also published *Berthing: A Poetry Workbook* (NEC/Virago, 1991), and was co-editor of *The New British Poetry* (Paladin, 1988).

From 2001 to 2003 she held a Royal Literary Fund Fellowship at Newcastle and Leeds Universities. She won the Northern Rock Foundation Writer's Award in 2005 and received a Cholmondeley Award in 2010. Since 1983 she has taught creative writing in a variety of contexts, mainly in adult education and as a writer in schools. In 2009/10 she held a writing residency with The Medical Foundation for the Care of Victims of Torture (now Freedom From Torture) in the North East, working with asylum seekers in Newcastle and Stockton. In 2013/14 she taught creative writing to undergraduates on the Poetry and Poetics course in the English Department of Durham University. She lives in Co. Durham.

Gillian Allnutt was awarded the Queen's Gold Medal for Poetry 2016. The Medal is given for excellence in poetry and was presented to her by The Queen.

# GILLIAN ALLNUTT

# wake

BLOODAXE BOOKS

ISBN: 978 1 78037 406 2

First published 2018 by
Bloodaxe Books Ltd,
Eastburn,
South Park,
Hexham,
Northumberland NE46 1BS.

www.bloodaxebooks.com
For further information about Bloodaxe titles
please visit our website or write to
the above address for a catalogue.

Supported using public funding by
ARTS COUNCIL
ENGLAND

Cover design: Neil Astley & Pamela Robertson-Pearce.

Printed in Great Britain by Bell & Bain Limited, Glasgow, Scotland, on
acid-free paper sourced from mills with FSC chain of custody certification.

*For Tom Midgley*

# ACKNOWLEDGEMENTS

Acknowledgements are due to the editors of the following publications in which some of these poems first appeared: *Beehive Poets 2015, Fanfare: an anthology of contemporary women's poetry* (Second Light Publications, 2015), *Hands & Wings: Poems for Freedom from Torture* (White Rat Press, 2015), *Her Wings of Glass: an anthology of contemporary women's poetry* (Second Light Publications, 2014), *Ploughshares, PN Review, Poetry, Poetry Ireland Review, The Poetry Review, Songs for the Unsung* (Grey Hen Press, 2017).

'Stars' appeared on the StAnza Poetry Festival website (www.stanzapoetry.org) in 2018.

Some of the poems were first published in *icumen* (Literal-Fish, 2014).

'lindisfarne: the roughs' was commissioned by Newcastle Centre for the Literary Arts for the Lindisfarne Poetry Project in 2013. It was published in *Shadow Script: Twelve Poems for Lindisfarne and Bamburgh* (NCLA, 2013) and recorded for an on-site sound installation in the summer of 2013. It was broadcast on the BBC Radio 4 programme *Lindisfarne: Poetry In Progress* in October 2014.

'The Word *Quire*' and 'Eliza Bowes' were commissioned by Durham University as a response to the exhibition *Hearing Voices: Suffering, Inspiration and the Everyday* held in Durham, November 2016–February 2017, in connection with the university's Wellcome Trust-funded interdisciplinary Hearing The Voice project.

# CONTENTS

## York Way

It happened to her. To her alone.
It didn't. He did it. On his own

in that bare room. You looked out on the railway line
at sidings. Not a train.

It looked as if Kings Cross had gone.
And London.

There was no announcement. And no platform
where she could have said goodbye to him.

## again

*(for John as ever)*


some people wear it in their shoulders you said
two shynesses


by the old lime kiln I sat down and ate my sandwiches
by the near


shored


you and I then
shriven


in my shoelessness fear of the Lord that fire and flet
unfit me for


*Lindisfarne, April 2013*

# lindisfarne: the roughs

### I

at thorn the wind that sore unshriven thing

### II

*anon*

in truth I was alone
as it had been corrack or coffin
I carried the earth, its poor inscription, on my back
who will remember it
who will remember the sun and the moon
my pillow stones

### III

silent the settlement of stone

### IV

*cuthbert alone*

*hwaet*
my whole assent, my heart, my hut
of stone unhewn and turf
and bent
*ferann*

V

or priory or prayer the wind blows through


VI

*in gertrude jekyll's garden*

am drawn, an old reluctance, like the moon

the sea, for example, sings to itself alone its *nunc dimittis*

we are bound to one another, God, my own anon

and of our solitude we are the guardian


VII

perpetual arrival of the sea and of the king acquisitive his people

# King Edward II

His body brought, accompanied, by abbot led, to Gloucester.

His effigy, alone, of alabaster

Made.

His bearded head.

His orb and sceptre and the lion his feet would rest upon.

His modesty.

His majesty.

His tomb-chest Purbeck-clad.

His canopy of local fine oolitic limestone made

By stonemasons from London.

# Grief

Stopped on the hard shoulder
blinded by –

Worlds in their otherness thundered by –

irresolute, there
by one another

not knowing or what to do

Began again
simply

went back on the motorway

entered Jerusalem, London, as if on a donkey
were for the time being OK

# Bookshop, London

*(for Mohamed Ben Madani)*


Man

from the Maghreb
at ebb.

Cache of the breath in the throat
in the thought of it –

*Maghreb*
from the verb

'to withdraw or depart'.
Taking in all of his stock at sunset

box after box of it
saying only of the work 'It is my sport'.

About the Tuareg, say
about the Sahara –

sough of the wind among stars
*Sahara*

'the Greatest Desert'.
Every morning putting himself out

there again
as if in

the Moroccan
sun.

It has steadied my heart
to know of that

man.

## Hereford Hop

*(for Tom)*


Meanwhile, I said, I have brought you a hundred grammes of
        Hereford Hop
from the expensive farm shop

at Stretton under Fosse
where the legions pass and pass

on their way from Bath
to Lutterworth.

Meanwhile, you said, according
to the Samsung

in the beginning
even kings

were led by the nose,
by the plosive

light of stars
that pales and passes, passes

as the soul upon its way
in perpetuity.

Who knows what
will come Hubbleward from the heart's

deep field,
from Cotswold

or from Bredon Hill?
Meanwhile

the table,
the makeshift vase, the improbable

orange blouse of the rose,
the cheese

without wine.
Imagine,

I said. Who knows
but we've rings on our fingers and bells on our toes?

## 1950s Childhood

Are you sitting comfortably, the wireless
asked us.
And we answered yes
as a matter of courtesy, of course.

## Among Women

*(for Tom)*

Waywardness

Or that in you I call Stromness –

They asked me in the corner shop

'Have you lost your husband? Have you given him the slip?'

Women of the Orkney biscuit

Business –

Even your Mum

For whom I bought some –

Shortbread flavoured with lemon –

Who asked me 'Are you an illusion?'

Liked them

Thought they were nice.

## 'O my chevalier!'

*(God to Man)*


man

my own


wild

rose of a world


least of all

spirit-levels


loess at your root

irresolute


in translation

alien some of the time as if stone

## Stranger

Who is this stranger lies here by me
Who, as my heart, has turned me over to God unheard?
Than my own words, stranger
Than my bed of words.

# Fleuve

*(for David Hart)*


'Word that, advisedly, will take the light and weight of water
        yesterday upon itself,
suffice me
with its vellum, verve.


'Word that will serve to make, by breaking, uniform the several
        surfaces of Severn
as I saw them yesterday
their light brown grey.


'What's credible cannot contain the heart's credulity
I know now.'


Thus I imagine Wulfstan
held


who'd helped to crown the Conqueror
and in the year 1084
would found,
build.


*fleuve:* (French) a large river

## abutment

but for the askance in her

but for the biding in abeyance of her

but for the clairvoyance that came to her like a grandmother

but for the expanse of love in her the lark in the clear air

but for the auld acquaintedness with violence in her

# the displaced child

as if belonging were imaginable element
and she inhabitant

and she a star
in ether

rather
as her mother's industrial sewing-machine once requisitioned for –

worsted she said whatever
as if she'd been there –

in Łódź she meant for the whole of the war –
and now there were neither lodgement nor entitlement for her

# Near the Peace Garden

*(for Lya Vollering)*


And in her heart in mine, exploded, over and over again, the

       Lancaster bomber.

*Somewhere, over Laon.*

It is uniform, the rain, though: it is always or April again.

*It was somewhere over Laon.*

It is August, Sunday afternoon.

I am walking with you in the garden of violated love,

of cabbages and rain,

and, with us, Anne Frank, Etty Hillesum,

their courage in our own

reiterative.


*Minsteracres Monastery, Co Durham*
*August 2012*


My mother's brother, an RAF navigator, was killed in action in April 1943.

# magdalen

the darkest hour

the stars arisen asinine

tomb and I left opened to the altogether

am I to live among men abandoned I may learn to love again

adrift in Jerusalem

am I upon strewn palm

## medlar, meditation

do not lay waste to, world in me, love

with your Christmas, bletted, of butter muslin, bone

with your bombing campaign above

Syria alone

without end, without asylum

*December 2015*

## 'as it were hunger...'

as it were hunger

happen

in my heart

as it were hunger

happen

in the king whose bare ship burial

in the pauper, then, whose kepier hospital

as I were one

in whom the hunger of the lord

might be laid down

a while a while and *yet a little while*

as it were hoard

# Stars

There are those who have not fled shame

the numberlessness of *am*

the innumerable one


in whom


the dark of the moon, as absence, abstinence, is home.

In shoals, in sheols, they will come

with mobile phones.


*Shalom.*


*Shalom:* (Hebrew) Hello; goodbye; peace

# Nearing Warminster

Salisbury, solitary, sings as if Isaiah in her –
*All Along the Watchtower* edge and ridge of plain they ride for
      Warminster.

Anger, broken in her, iron age, stone age, bone and barrow, is as if her
Father yet not father photographed before the war
Unfathomed by her –

Anger of another relatively new to her beside her now
Like coulter – plough-hard, harrow-hard –
Would break the clod of her

For what is yet unheard in her is hoard
It is for him to bare.

As if the solitary village in her, commandeered, were Imber
Unrestored –

As if the word *abide with me* were loud and overlord in her.

*Imber*, a village on Salisbury Plain taken over by the army in 1943, is still
uninhabited today.

# belsen

*(in memory of my father)*


heard them, hut- and bone-hoard, when he neared me to him

hid the need of them, the unremembered, from him

midden I am

# music

*ruach*

breath umbilical

'the lark in the clear air'

common

ecuelle

*ruach:* (Hebrew) breath, wind, spirit

# early spring

am without anger wounded

poetry Bashō's rare paper raincoat burned

I stand

as ash by winter bound

as crow stoned

as heron sudden
land

by absence astounded
by presence astounded

# The Quince Tree

grows often to the height and bigness of a reasonable apple tree

crooked, with a rough bark, spreading arms, and branches far abroad

the leaves [...] not dented at all about the edges

the flowers [...] sometimes dashed over with a blush

the fruit that follows [...] being [...] covered with a white freeze,
       or cotton [...]

bunched out oftentimes in some places,

some being like an apple, and some a pear

The above being taken from *Culpeper's Complete Herbal* (1653)

# Song

I remember it yet
as Carterhaugh
my own green mantle
my life

older than laughter
than fear
its light root
in air

in haar
abroad
unbidden
as a bird

recalled me
common
comely
to my own

Tam Lin

# Prodigal

Here you are then,

not at all before the appointed time,

looking out of a dining-room window at a dark red rhododendron.

What a long time love has been rowing itself home.

## 'We have tret one another...'

We have tret one another to the tendered brutalities –
rough sometimes as the waters of Tyne met head-on under
    Warden Hill –
that if not for the boatman and his half-forgotten dialect
would have left the heart without avail.

# in a field of oats

the wind says 'mississippi' or 'persepolis' or 'erysipelas'
the yellowhammer 'little bit of bread and no cheese'
but who will hear us

now
our 'ich und du'

the world for all its wild percussive way
will come upon us wordlessly
among the rows

*Wooler, Northumberland*
*August 2015*

*ich und du:* (German) I and thou

## silence

the poet, discalceate

## prayer

impromptu

of the hour

the heart

old heretic

old whore

exemplary

*en forme de poire*

*en forme de poire:* (French) pear-shaped. A piano piece by Erik Satie.

## meditation

the rain intent
rough tetter of it on the slate roof, slant
the out and out of it

tetter of thought
the rat skitterfoot
*He hath scattered* –

imagination only
mantle of me as I thought
*I want to do it my own*

held out, then, for the least elaboration of the heart
the *Liber Eliensis* of the heart
lost Cratendune

for now the evermantle of anon
the tent and the attent of it
by which I am –

there is this, then, the rain extant

# The Word *Quire*


come to me as I stand quietly here

come to me now from I know not where –

*The wind blows where it wills, and you hear the sound thereof, but*

*can not tell from where it came, and where –*

come to me, Julian with her *poor unlettered creature*


God come with her: Maker, Keeper, Lover

*But what he is who is in truth... I cannot tell –*

who was not in the little thing he showed her –

*the size of a hazelnut, on the palm of my hand, round like a ball –*

not in the nutshell of her

thought – though he as thought surrounded her


As I sit thinking with a pencil on a piece of paper

so she there or other

scribe some half a century later

sat with quill, with ink of oak gall, with a measured quire

# my seventeenth-century heart

wherein

    no hoard

       but God

          whose bare upholstery

             whose throne of wood

# haunt


fire and flet, quiet customary, what they could afford

horsehair the sofa

half-remembered

by her

whose heart, unmitigated, magnified the Lord

old harrier


*Haworth Parsonage, March 2014*

Refusing to give in to illness and go to bed, Emily Brontë died, in December 1848, lying on the sofa downstairs.

# Portrait of Hester by her husband

How well she has worn the wooden evangelist of the mind
I wrought in her.

He is fraught as Angel Clare
With honesty, with his *latchet*
Worthy of her.

When I am gone she will put him on the fire
As if he'd condemned her.

# Harnham

*(for Deborah)*

stars afield

    whose laughter we have failed

        to let fall

            gruff or guttural

                into the heart's begging-bowl

night-long the farm machinery continues with its generation

we, afield

    half afraid of the bull

        by whose bellowing our bluff is called

            our conversation all

                about Simone Weil

*Harnham Buddhist Monastery, Northumberland, November 2014*

## prayer

may I make amendment

not in the mind –
Le Corbusier's *machine for living in*
his signed environment –

but in the tent or tabernacle of the heart
*à l'abri* –

allowing of all worlds only the wind
for wall

*à l'abri de:* (French) sheltered or screened from (something)

# desuetude

*(for Tom)*


your crowd of jamjars

like asylum seekers

set aside for

cumin, say, or cardamom or coriander

as they were samovars

survivors

of war

there are bluebirds over

there you are

where we are now among all these computers waiting for repair


*August 2015*

## considering

the dear improbability of cricket on the radio
of you

# Home

*(for Tom)*

How beautiful you are when you do not understand me.
I turn on my heel, remembering, say 'I will see'
and, in my mind's ear, hear my old asylum-seeking Fetle say
'I back, I back'.
Back from her own far country
where she wasn't detained
and didn't die.

# My Competence

*(for Tom)*

Look at my hands of horn and leather.

The rough and ready of them.

Men for all seasons.

Weather-vanes.

I have laid them down in the lap of this Sunday morning's sun.

My being with you in love will mantle me from the predations of

　　　　other men and women

And my own.

# Going to Gloucester

*(for Tom)*


In Cheltenham.

Well then.

Even the police station a cordial Cotswold stone.

How well I shall weather.

Wifedom.

Martha who comes to me now in her apron.

In a shower of rain.

How English I am.

# Wedding-dress

*(for Laura)*

Once we were here or was it there, our sister ourself, mysteriously.

Where the moon was, exactly.

Now there are only the printed instructions on packets to make
out, patiently.

Let us be quiet, once more, like the sea.

The accumulated incidental knowledge of the sea.

Let there be marriage-lines too small to know of nakedly.

Let the law be kept within its one and only.

Let there be, about us, with us, always.

Something we didn't quite manage to say.

Didn't say.

# Elias

I am always Elias, though I am a woman and not a prophet. I am always thin, always dry, and so I was as a child. When I was a girl of 12 and my body was an awkward wrist, one that had been broken too badly ever to grow back other than wrily, awry, I was walking according to my wont in the wild barley grass at the edge of my father's field and, though I was tall, at that time of late summer the grass came up to my shoulders. I walked sideways, looking. And I found grandmother's foot. I call it that. My father insisted it was a last. His brother, estranged, had cobbled. It was in another village and I never knew him. But the foot with its wooden limp belonged to my grandmother, invented, who sprang up out of the grass into being at once. She limped along home behind me and I had to slow down, though I was hungry and I knew she must be too. There was nettle soup I had made in the early morning and some of Bessarabia's old black bread in the bin. That would do. With water out of the jug, straight out of the jug. I could see where grandmother's foot joined her leg, it hurt. But I asked her where she was born and she only said on the road between the one hill and the other. And there was never a van and never a cart and now and then a donkey or a frame on a wheel but mostly bundles on backs and shoulders, bundles in tweed, and I saw she was bent as she limped along. She wore a dull blue blouse and a long grey skirt of some poor stuff, a foreign cloth. I asked if she came in a boat and she said of course she did, everyone comes in a boat to be born, and I said I didn't and anyway what about the hills you were born between? The sea was between the hills, she said and closed her eyes and her wooden foot crushed the small flowers in the way.

# Ignominy

Withal I know the lovely lone laboriousness of being

like cloud in the making.

I stand, alone, mistaken

in undress.

The crows erupt, like words, around me –

*Lord, Lord –*

with all their raucousness.

## Eliza Bowes

Though they say she was not, I imagine her quiet.
As a clean petticoat or placket.

As the dry aqueduct
of the heart.

Polite.

Less so the warders – those whose words
authoritative, swart
abducted her aloud.

*An imbecile of moderate grade.*

I imagine her safe in the silence of retreat
in the soft restraint shirt
they put on her.

Look at the swathe of it.

Look at the sleeves, sewn shut.

In which her own hands must have faltered, felt for one another,
    fallen quiet.
Each in its holt alone and lithe.

## birthday

come with the snow, my butterfly girl, my bicycle girl

    as a flock of girls in flight over the wooden-floored hotel

        as to Mary in her plight the angel Gabriel


who can say who she


for now is quiet and thick and still


come with the snow, unmistakable girl in her metal chair with its

    wooden wheels

    as a lonely regatta

        as to me, in thought, my soul


who can say


*my name is Mauthausen: for we are many*


*January 2013*

## Predictive Text

I want no more to do with what is understandable.

There there.

Only the lilliburlero of bird because it is songful.
The lark ascending the air.

Vaughan Williams' Surrey local choir of ladies sorrowful between the wars.

Only the dot and carry one of Clare who gave himself moon and stars
to Northampton County Asylum
to the cruelty and kindness of others.

*El Cant dels Ocells* or Song of the Birds or Pau Casals' dear Catalan.

Only the worn confabulation of the Wooden Queen among Moomins
her lolling in the water
like Ophelia.

La la.

## 'Light will come anyway...'

Light will come anyway
momentarily
or like snow will lie
a while.

# healing

*(for my father)*


now, unquestionable
as the heart
its *mysterium tremendum*
its horse and cart

now, and I able
as Tapio, couth, uncouth
to take you in, father,
your handful of cold earth

now, and you
as forester will know –
and Sibelius knew –
*the smell of the first snow*

# The King's Men

Slough my father's anger from me as it were an old skin
of my own.

Plough it in-
to cotswold, layered down-

land of imperial leather, dark tan
roan

where all the kings all the king's men
as standing-stones

as veterans
of *The Old Playboys' Association*

stiff in their bones
lie down

half lying down
like bathers in Cézanne.

# Beech in Lineover Wood

Patient

in silent possession of the soul –

soul of the world and of Cotswold –


Ancient

most ancient of trees and days

some old Caliban in us could call upon –


The path is narrow and small and, rising, goes among grasses –

*as we forgive them that trespass against us –*

in its own way


poor

as our own.

O Prospero, what kings we are in the common solemnity of late

        afternoon.


*Cotswold Way, Gloucestershire*
*July 2014*

# Amplitude

May Lord be lived in me

as Orford Ness
a certain landedness
what's promised

in disclosure, that of stone
the progress of the moon
the promiscuity of Mary Magdalen

May I be opened as the heart alone is quietly

as *sumer is icumen in*
as cope-chest
to the cerement and ceremonial of all

May Love be lived in me

as *loosed upon the world*
as linenfold

# wake

*(for my father, myself)*


solitude laid down

as bedrock, being –

sweet chariot, sweet clarinet, of bone

where late the sweet bird sang –

# NOTES

**again** (11): The phrase 'fire and flet' can be found in 'The Lyke-Wake Dirge'. 'Flet' means houseroom; the floor or ground beneath one's feet; a dwelling, house or hall; the inner part of a house.

**lindisfarne: the roughs** (12): II. A local man, a native of Northumbria, recalls an earlier time of his life when he was converted from the pagan religion to Christianity by Aidan and a group of Irish monks who came from Iona to Lindisfarne in 634. Pillow stones are small stones laid flat on the surface of a grave, inscribed with a cross and the name of the person buried there. IV, VII. Cuthbert (*c.* 635–687) retired in 676 from the monastic community on Lindisfarne to a hermitage on Farne Island where he spent nine years in prayer and contemplation. In 685 King Egfrid of Northumbria arrived to ask him to become Bishop of Lindisfarne. Reluctantly he consented but within two years returned to his hermitage where he died. 'Hwaet' is an Anglo-Saxon word, an exclamation made at the beginning of a poem or speech to call for attention. 'Ferann', a Celtic word meaning 'land', gave rise to the name Farne. VI: Gertrude Jekyll planned the planting of the old walled garden belonging to the castle on Lindisfarne around 1911. It is still a garden, a sheltered enclosure on the exposed headland, a safe place in which to sit and listen to the sea. The Nunc Dimittis is a prayer from the service of evensong in the Anglican Church, named after the opening words of the prayer in Latin. The words form the Song of Simeon in Luke 2.29-32.

**King Edward II** (14): Edward II was king of England from 1307 to 1327 when he was deposed and imprisoned in Berkeley Castle where he died. John Thokey, Abbot of Gloucester, received instructions to accompany the former king's body to Gloucester. A state funeral took place in the cathedral in December 1327 but it was not until 1329 that Edward III came to Gloucester to plan the construction of an ornate tomb fit for his father.

**Hereford Hop** (18): This is the name of a local cheese coated in toasted hops. The Roman road Fosse Way ran between Axminster and Lincoln; modern roads follow the route of it. Bredon Hill in

Worcestershire is celebrated in A.E. Housman's poem of that name and in settings by several composers including Ralph Vaughan Williams. The Hubble Ultra-Deep Field is an image of a small region of space in the constellation Fornax, composited from Hubble Space Telescope data accumulated over a period from 24 September 2003 through to 16 January 2004. Looking back approximately 13 billion years (between 400 and 800 million years after the Big Bang) it will be used to search for galaxies that existed at that time. The image contains an estimated 10,000 galaxies. (Wikipedia)

**1950s Childhood** (20): The programme *Listen with Mother* ran on BBC radio from 1950 to 1982. Each day the story was introduced with the words 'Are you sitting comfortably? Then I'll begin.'

**'O my chevalier!'** (22): The title is a quotation from 'The Windhover' by Gerard Manley Hopkins.

**Fleuve** (24): As Bishop of Worcester from 1062 to 1095, Wulfstan was the only English-born bishop to retain his diocese for any significant time after the Norman Conquest. A social reformer, he struggled to bridge the gap between the old and new regimes and to alleviate the suffering of the poor.

**the displaced child** (26): Łódź is known as 'the Polish Manchester'. Its textile industry was kept going through World War II. Its Jewish cemetery is the largest in Europe.

**Near the Peace Garden** (27): Like Anne Frank (1929-45), Etty Hillesum (1914-43) spent much of World War II living in Amsterdam. The story of her extraordinary, accelerated spiritual journey and the work she did among her fellow Jews during the Holocaust is told in *An Interrupted Life: The Diaries and Letters of Etty Hillesum 1941–43*, published in English translation by Persephone Books London in 1999 and elsewhere.

**medlar, meditation** (29): 'Bletting' is a process of softening beyond ripening that medlars undergo to make them edible. They are often made into medlar jelly.

**'as it were hunger...'** (30): Kepier Hospital was founded as an alms-house in Durham in the 12th century. 'yet a little while' are words spoken by Jesus at John 7.33 and elsewhere in that Gospel.

**Stars** (31): Sheol is the Hebrew abode of the dead or departed spirits.

**belsen** (33): In May 1945 my father's flame-throwing tank regiment was ordered to take part in burning down Belsen after the camp had been cleared. My father never spoke of it.

**early spring** (35): In preparation for the journey described in *The Records of a Travel-worn Satchel* the Japanese poet Bashō (1644–94) packed, among other things, a paper raincoat.

**'We have tret one another...'** (39): The North and South Tyne meet at Warden Hill in Northumberland. 'The Waters of Tyne' is a love song from the North East of England.

**in a field of oats** (40): *Ich und Du* by Martin Buber was first published in English translation as *I and Thou* in 1937.

**meditation** (43): 'He hath scattered the proud in the imagination of their hearts' is from The Magnificat, Luke 1.51. 'I want to do it my own' is something I apparently said very often as a young child. The *Liber Eliensis* is a 12th-century English chronicle and history written in Latin at Ely Abbey, which became Ely Cathedral in 1109. It covers the period from the founding of the abbey in 673 until the middle of the 12th century. Cratendune is the name of the lost village reported in that chronicle.

**The Word *Quire*** (44): On 8 May 1373 Julian of Norwich (1342–1416) received 16 'shewings' or visions of Christ on the cross. She spent the remainder of her life as a 'recluse atte Norwyche', writing both short and long accounts of this mystical experience and her meditations on it. The exhibition *Hearing Voices: Suffering, Inspiration and the Everyday*, shown in Durham (November 2016 – February 2017) included the only surviving original of the short text in a manuscript from 1450. The poem came to me as I looked at this ms. The quotation in line 3 is from John 3.8 in the King James Bible translation of 2000. Other quotations are from Julian's own *Revelations of Divine Love*, translated by Clifton Wolters and published in Penguin Classics, 1966.

**haunt** (46): For 'fire and flet' see note to the poem 'again' (11).

**Portrait of Hester by her husband** (47): Angel Clare is from Hardy's *Tess of the D'Urbervilles*. For 'latchet' see Luke 3.16.

**prayer** (49): *À l'abri de rien*, a novel by Olivier Adam, was originally published in 2007 and is concerned with asylum seekers living in 'the Jungle' at Calais.

**desuetude** (50): Tom, to whom the poem is addressed, runs a computer repair business from his house.

**Home** (52): Fetle is a friend and erstwhile asylum seeker for whom – in spite of her holding British citizenship – there is always a risk in visiting her own country.

**Ignominy** (57): *Lord, Lord:* Matthew 7.21.

**Eliza Bowes** (58): On 18 August 1914, Eliza Bowes – an 18-year-old girl from Houghton-le-Spring in County Durham – was committed to the Winterton Hospital, the county asylum. On her admission she was described as a 'moderate grade imbecile' and noted to be noisy, restless and continually crying. She was hearing voices which were calling her names; she also had epileptic fits which became more frequent over time. She died at Winterton on 2 October 1915. In the exhibition *Hearing Voices: Suffering, Inspiration and the Everyday*, shown in Durham (November 2016–February 2017), there was a photo of Eliza Bowes and a note about her. Other exhibits included the sort of 'soft restraint shirt' she might have been put in to quiet her – a garment thick, padded and heavy which would have enclosed her hands in the sleeves.

**birthday** (59): *for we are many:* Mark 5.9.

**healing** (62): *Mysterium tremendum:* the experience of the numinous as defined and explored by German philosopher and theologian Rudolf Otto (1869–1937) in his book *The Idea of the Holy*. Tapio is a forest spirit or god in Finnish and Norse mythology who figures prominently in the *Kalevala*. *Tapiola* (1926) is a tone poem by Jean Sibelius. Of his own Sixth Symphony Sibelius wrote, in 1943, that 'it always reminds me of the scent of the first snow'.

**The King's Men** (63): The Rollright Stones is a complex of three

Neolithic and Bronze Age megalithic monuments standing, near the village of Long Compton, high above the surrounding countryside on the borders of Oxfordshire and Warwickshire. The monuments are known as the King Stone, the King's Men and the Whispering Knights: the first is a single monolith; the second, a stone circle; the third, the remains of a burial chamber with four surviving standing 'stones leaning together around a fifth recumbent stone. *The Old Playboys' Association:* as one of the Old Playboys, my father was reunited with the men he had fought with in the Second World War, veterans of The Buffs and fellow crew members of the flame-throwing tank in which he had served.

**Amplitude** (65): *sumer is icumen in* is from 'The Cuckoo Song', sometimes said to be the earliest English poem, and *loosed upon the world* is from W.B. Yeats's poem 'The Second Coming'.